Fill Me *or* Kill Me...

JUST DON'T LEAVE ME THE WAY I AM

Joel & Linda Budd

CROSSSTAFF
PUBLISHERS, LLC

Fill Me or Kill Me...Just Don't Leave Me the Way I Am
ISBN 0-9743876-2-2
Copyright © 2007 by Joel & Linda Budd
1439 East 71st Street
Tulsa, OK 74136

Printed in the United States of America.

Dedication

We dedicate this story to all those humble, nameless, faceless people who serve on prayer teams where God is pouring out His Spirit on people. We thank you for praying countless hours for us to receive more of the Father's love, even when you didn't know us or didn't know what the Holy Spirit was doing in us. God has used you to lift people like us higher, so He could heal us deeper and take us way beyond where we would have gone on our own. As you soak others in prayer and let the Holy Spirit flow through you to bless others, you are raising the water level of God's presence, anointing, and love in hungry, thirsty hearts. You have sown to the Spirit and we pray now for you to reap from the Spirit, "More, Lord!"

Acknowledgements

We want to thank all those who helped with our story, this book, and the spiritual and physical process behind it.

Thank you, precious daughters Cristin, Joelle, and Haley, for living through all of this story and more with us — and changing with us.

Thank you, church family of Open Bible Fellowship, for sticking with us and loving us through these years of visitation and transformation. The new wine is better with friends like you! You are the best drinking buddies a couple of pastors could ever ask for.

Thank you, John and Carol Arnott and the members of the Toronto Airport Church, for making a place for strangers like us to come and experience the Father's affection and the Holy Spirit's indescribable manifest presence. You found the pearl, bought the field, and have been a father and mother to many "orphans" who needed to experience the

Spirit of adoption like us. This generation has been and is still being changed by your humble service.

Thank you, Scott Kaste, for patiently walking us through the process of getting this done. It literally would not have happened without you.

To Jeannie Cozad for all the transcribing and Elizabeth Sherman for your skills and gifts, you have added much to make this possible. Thank you and bless you.

Thank You, Holy Spirit, for being gracious to us and for giving us a new hunger and thirst for more of God when we didn't even know enough to be hungry.

Table of Contents

Foreword

Fill Me or Kill Me is a gripping title that reflects the desperate heart cry for God that can come to people when the pressures of life are piled on to the breaking point. Many will identify with pain and tragedy and what has been called "the long, dark night of the soul." The question really is, how will you react to it? Will this make you bitter or better? Will you press into God for your breakthrough, or will you go down in defeat?

In the midst of successful church growth, a sudden and unexpected family tragedy stopped Joel and Linda Budd in their tracks. "God, where are You?" "Where were You?" "God, we need You now!" became the desperate cry of their hearts.

Funny, isn't it, that when the serious realities of life crash in upon us, we can no longer "play church" and carry on in our complacency. These pastors, first separately and then together, began to long for that which is real. They became desperate for the reality of God, for the presence of God. And God has promised, hasn't He, that when you seek Him with all of your heart, you will find Him. (See Jeremiah 29:13.)

This book tells the story of Joel and Linda Budd's life-changing, over-the-top, wonderful, glorious encounter with the living God, which — of course — totally changed their lives forever. It tells how their family relationships became enriched and alive again. It shares the mystery of how (believe it or not) many of their friends and church folks didn't like what happened to them and chose to distance themselves. It tells how their anointing for ministry has gone from insipid to powerful with miracles, signs, and wonders happening on an ever-increasing basis.

Their church is growing again, but this time the lost, the lonely, the broken, the sick, and the hurting are finding that Jesus Christ is the powerful answer they were looking for.

John Arnott
Founding Pastor
Toronto Airport Christian Fellowship

Introduction

This is a testimony of being transformed and transfigured by the Holy Spirit (Romans 12:1-2). It's our subjective experience — not deep — but deeply personal. We recount our pathway to experiencing God in dimensions of love, power, and deliverance that were new to us. We experienced Him in ways we never dreamed of or thought possible — or necessary.

Our desire is that the spiritual dynamic behind our testimony of Jesus would happen for you too. "For the testimony of Jesus is the spirit of prophecy" (Revelation 19:10). We understand this to mean that an anointed testimony about what Jesus has done or is doing in one life can release prophetic waves of fresh grace to flow into the life of another spiritually hungry, receptive heart.

We have seen in God's Word and by personal experience that it's always the right time for new wineskins. We didn't know that we needed to become new wineskins again (to carry a fresh, new wine in a new season of time on God's calendar). We thought we were being the new wineskin. We didn't realize that every new wineskin needs to keep becoming new in new seasons of God's Spirit. The truth is, if you don't change and grow, often in the spirit, you harden without knowing it and the new wineskin becomes the old wineskin, not continually preparing and coming full circle for the next move of God's Spirit.

As a married couple and co-pastors of a church, we both have experienced different facets of the same story. The chapters are written in first person, so it may be Joel sharing or it may be Linda sharing. To make it easier for you, under each chapter title we placed a name in parentheses so you can tell who is writing. We pray this testimony of Jesus working in us will be used in some way by the Holy Spirit to kiss your heart awake to new levels of the Father's affection for you.

CHAPTER 1

Fill Me or Kill Me

(JOEL)

I was in desperate need of personal revival —
but I did not know it. Don't miss what I just said!
You can be in desperate need of something more
from the Holy Spirit and not know it. I was pastoring a thriving, growing church. I thought I had
everything I needed, but I had no clue.

Our church had begun with a few people in a
home and graduated to a movie theater. Then my
wife Linda and I attended a church-growth seminar,
worked very hard to apply what we had learned, and
broke through the 200-member barrier. Shortly after

that we received a note that said, "Congratulations on breaking the 200-member barrier! Now you need our seminar on how to break the 400-member barrier. Only a small percentage of churches in America get invited to this seminar."

Off we went to the next seminar to learn more principles of church growth. We came home fired up, worked incredibly hard to implement and carry out everything we learned, and it wasn't long before we were running four hundred members. Then we got another letter in the mail, saying, "Congratulations! You have broken the 400-member barrier! Now you need our seminar on how to break the 800-member barrier. Only a small percentage of churches in America get invited to this seminar."

The hard work continued until one day we got a phone call. They said, "Congratulations on breaking the 800-member barrier! Now you need our seminar on how to break the 1100-member barrier. Only a small percentage of churches in America get invited to this seminar. And guess what? We are going to fly you to Palm Springs for a free seminar!"

Just as I was about to fall into old habits and get excited, I heard my heart say, "I don't want to do this anymore." It suddenly hit me that this was not what I had signed up for. I was running around like a crazy man and getting no fulfillment from what others were calling success. This realization stopped me in my tracks, and it was at this point that *my spiritual eyes began to open — my first step toward personal revival.* I saw our church for what it was. Nobody was getting saved, nobody was getting healed, nobody was getting delivered, and I couldn't find the harvest to save my life!

We were producing nice dramas, which would cause believers from other churches to come to our church. We had a great worship leader, singers, and band; so believers who loved good worship music would leave their churches and join ours. Our youth and children's departments were fun and exciting, so people from other churches would come over to our church so their kids could have a good time. Basically, we were just enticing believers from other churches to come to our church. We were also attracting believers who had been offended and hurt at other churches and had become disconnected from the body of Christ.

My eyes were opened to the fact that all our hard work was primarily doing nothing more than stealing sheep, that we couldn't find the harvest of souls if our lives depended upon it. All that hard work and all those long hours amounted to nothing. It was straw.

> For no one can lay any foundation other than the one already laid, which is Jesus Christ. If any man builds on this foundation using gold, silver, costly stones, wood, hay or straw, his work will be shown for what it is, because the Day will bring it to light. It will be revealed with fire, and the fire will test the quality of each man's work.
>
> 1 Corinthians 3:11-13

The Bible tells us that the quality of our works will get the fire test. All our works will be put on God's heavenly altar. The works built on the foundation of Jesus Christ will be gold, silver, and precious stones; they will not burn but will bring eternal rewards. The works not built upon Jesus Christ will be wood, hay, or straw. They will be burned as worthless to God's kingdom.

Looking back, not everything we did in those years was bad. We helped a lot of disconnected believers get reconnected in church. We were very respectful of people and helped them in their relationships. We encouraged everyone to love each other and care for one another. There was no hype, and we met in a warehouse, which people thought was cool because it was not a religious atmosphere.

We also tried our best to be completely honest and transparent. When we had marriage problems, we spent a year in counseling, dealt with our dysfunctional communication, and then brought our counselor to the congregation on a Sunday morning and gave our testimony. We wanted other couples who were having trouble to learn what we had learned. We did a lot of counseling, and many believers were encouraged.

Our church was popular with students and young couples, but they were there to be encouraged and built up to go out and be a success in life. Many of them were not interested in knowing God intimately. They wanted biblical principles to get where they wanted to go in their jobs and to be happy in their families. There was nothing wrong with that, but again, there was a real lack of intimacy with God, no powerful move of the Spirit — and little interest in seeing the lost saved.

At that moment in time when my eyes were opened, I saw myself standing before the Lord on that Day. On the altar of God were a few pieces of gold, silver, and precious stones — and a bonfire — that revealed my service to Him.

CHAPTER 2

Trains and Planes

(JOEL)

Although we were having what appeared to many as great success with a growing church, I was empty and tired, and not just because of all the hard work in the church. During a Christmas vacation, a terrible thing had happened to our family. Our four-year-old daughter Joelle was raped, and I experienced the horror of a father whose family was viciously attacked right before his eyes. It was the most terrifying time of my life. Although it was over in a matter of days, by the time we got home, we were devastated. When we turned to the elders of our church, because Joelle was so young, they advised us to try to forget about it and to never talk about it. Not knowing what else to do, we agreed.

Linda kept going, doing everything she had always done, but she had lost her zeal. Looking back, I see that I suppressed all my feelings and threw myself into the ministry to escape. Every now and then the painful memory would pop up, and I would cry out, "Why, Lord? Why did this happen to us when we were doing all we could for You?" When I heard nothing, I stuffed it again and turned my focus fully on whatever task was at hand. I worked even harder to see the church grow, but any enjoyment of life I had had was gone. This led to the second step on my pathway to personal revival, and it had nothing to do with my goodness, my intelligence, or my spirituality. Jesus was answering my cries for help. I just didn't know it.

The second step on my pathway to personal revival was the Holy Spirit rising up in me and inciting hunger and thirst. God's grace had already opened my eyes to see how I was throwing every bit of energy into something that didn't come close to hitting the target I believed He had set for me. Now His grace began to touch my life in another way. I began to get hungry and thirsty. I did not know that my hunger and thirst was a move of the Holy Spirit, that I didn't have enough sense to be hungry and thirsty! It was His goodness and mercy that did this.

Then this hunger and thirst, this longing of the Spirit within me, created a desperation in my own spirit and I began to groan. I had never groaned in the Spirit in my whole life, but I began to groan and cry out for Him. At the same time my rational mind began searching for something that would express what I was experiencing. Over and over, the only thought that would emerge from all this groaning and crying was, "Holy Spirit, fill me or kill me, but don't leave me this way."

My whole life began to change. I went on long fasts. I took long prayer walks. I would be in the middle of a meeting or working in my office and this longing would literally overwhelm me. It was so great at times that I just had to leave! I'd get in my car and groan and cry and say over and over, "Holy Spirit, fill me or kill me, but don't leave me this way." Today I believe that this is something all of us need on a regular basis to refire our spirits and keep us on track with what God really wants for our lives.

The next thing that began to come out of my mouth was, "There's got to be more, Lord. There's got to be more than what I have, more than this level that I live at with You." When you begin to pray things like, "Fill me or kill me" and "There's got to be more," you know that something in you has got to die because something new has to come forth. You are going to have to change, give up some things — and it often feels like you are throwing yourself off a cliff.

Our church was known in Tulsa as "the safe church." We considered that to be a great compliment. Nothing weird or controversial ever happened at our church. Counseling clinics in town would send their people to Open Bible Fellowship because it was safe. We were "seeker sensitive," and everything that happened during our services was easily explained and calm. Unfortunately, even demons knew we were a safe church. They probably spread the word, "Hey, get on somebody who goes to Open Bible Fellowship. Nothing will happen to you over there. It's safe."

If you had observed our church back then, you would have described it the same way commercials described light beer: tastes great, less filling. Today we look back and refer to our church then as "Church Light." From time to time when the worship music was really affecting me, I would raise my hands just a little bit — lightly. Standing on the front row at the beginning of each service, I did nothing to draw attention to myself. Everything was *light*.

One Sunday night we were having this nice, safe worship service at Church Light. I had told nobody about this hunger and thirst that was happening to me. I was moved by the worship music and lifted my hands very *lightly* as usual, when all of a sudden I found myself in an open vision. If you have never had an open vision before, it is like you are really someplace else.

Suddenly, I was standing on railroad tracks, and I began to look around, saying, "How did I get here?" Then I looked down the railroad tracks and saw an old, huge, black locomotive charging straight for me. The smoke was coming out of the smokestack because it was one of those late nineteenth century trains, and sparks and steam and all kinds of noises were flying out from it.

I thought, *I guess I better get off the tracks.* Then I realized I could not move my legs! No matter how hard I tried, my feet would not come off the tracks. I was horrified as the train moved closer and closer and began to blow its whistle over and over, like it was yelling, "Get off the tracks, Stupid! We're going to kill you!" But I still couldn't move.

I began to cry, "Oh God, help me! Help me!" It never occurred to me that I had been praying for six months now, "God, fill me or kill me."

An open vision is not like a prophetic picture, where you see it in your mind and say, "Thank You, God. That's really great." In an open vision everything seems so real, you are really there, and you are really experiencing what your senses are perceiving. So by now I was screaming, crying, and acting like a total coward. In fact, I'm surprised I didn't wet my pants. "Oh God, help me! Help me!"

Just as the train was about to hit me, I heard a voice. I will never forget this as long as I live. It said, "Hello, I'm the Holy Spirit. I would like to come to your church."

The vision was over and there I was, standing in front of Church Light with my hands slightly lifted. Pretending that nothing had happened, I tried to pull myself together. I could find no rational explanation for what I had just experienced, and I certainly couldn't explain it to anyone else. I was so shaken that afterward I stopped praying, "Fill me or kill me." In fact, I didn't say a word to God because I knew that if the Holy Spirit came to my church, I would die.

Many of us cry out for more of God and want to go from where we are to the "next level." However, very few of us really want to die to ourselves to do it, and we don't want to leave the comfort of familiar spiritual atmospheres, habits, relationships, and religious routines. We don't want to crucify the flesh that needs to die in order for us to grow up in the Lord. Thus, for a whole week I didn't pray, worship, or do anything remotely spiritual. I was scared. I knew that something terrible was about to happen to me.

After that week passed, being careful to engage in absolutely no spiritual activity at all, I began to recover and feel more at ease. At the next Sunday night service at Church Light, I was standing in my usual place. The worship music was nice and light.

Everything was familiar, comfortable, and safe when suddenly I was in another open vision.

This time I was standing on a mountain, like the one in the opening scene of the movie, *The Sound of Music!* I thought, *This is beautiful. Awesome. Gorgeous.* I ran my hand over the knee-high grass, the sky was a beautiful shade of blue, and I could see the valleys surrounding the hill. Just when I thought about worshipping, I saw this airplane in the distance. It looked okay and didn't disturb me, but then it turned in my direction.

As it got closer, I saw it more clearly. I thought to myself, *That's a World War II P-51 Mustang.* (I'm a World War II buff.) This plane was known as "the tank buster." It was not only designed for combat, but also it carried tank buster rockets under the wings.

Then I realized that because I was on a mountaintop the airplane was eye-level with me, and I knew it was headed straight for me in an all-out

27

attack. Before I could do anything there were missiles exploding and bullets flying all around me, but I couldn't move! Then the plane shot off the tank busters, and I saw one missile coming right towards me. It was going to hit me and blow me to smithereens because I was paralyzed and could not move. I knew I was about to die. Suddenly everything froze and I heard a voice say, "Hello, I'm the Holy Spirit. I would like to come to your church."

CHAPTER 3

What Have I Done?!!!

(JOEL)

The vision ended and there I was back at Church Light, standing on the front row. But before I had time to think about it a lady in our church walked up to me and tapped me on the shoulder. She said, "Pastor, I feel like I have a tongue and an interpretation." Now that didn't happen very often at Church Light, but I thought, *It's Sunday night. That's safe.* I handed her the microphone and said, "As soon as the music stops, just go up front and give the word."

The music ended. She stepped up to the pulpit. She gave a nice little tongue. Suddenly I thought,

Oh no. If the Holy Spirit comes I am going to die. Then I heard the strangest interpretation of a tongue I had ever heard. "Hello. I am the Holy Spirit, and I am God. I want to come to your church, and I want to come in My way. I want to come in power. I want to be Myself in your church. Will you let Me come? Will you let Me come? Will you let Me come?"

A few people in the congregation responded, "Bless God!" But I was thinking to myself, *Oh you fool! Now they are all saying how nice it would be for the Holy Spirit to come because you taught them He is a gentleman, which is what you were taught. You taught them He would never embarrass them or make them uncomfortable in any way. But if He comes, they will know that you didn't tell them the truth. They will find out that He's like a freight train or a tank buster!*

I didn't know what to do. I could hear some of them softly crying, "Yes, Holy Spirit. Come, little dove!" They were like little cooing birds calling to the One they thought of as a sweet little dove, when I knew He was really an aggressive, powerful attack aircraft!

Because I had always had a fear of man and had to have people's acceptance, I did the stupidest thing I had ever done. I took the microphone and said, "Okay, you heard the tongue and interpretation, and you heard that the Holy Spirit would like to come. So we are going to take a vote. All those who are in favor of the Holy Spirit coming the way He wants to come, raise your right hand." I decided that if I was going down, I was not going down alone!

About two-thirds of the people raised their hands. I said, "Okay, it looks like over two-thirds of you have voted for the Holy Spirit to come. I'm president of this corporation, so I declare it unanimous." I told the men to come to the front and stand on one side and the women to come to the front and stand on the other side. When the first gentleman to come forward was nearly to the front, I stretched out my hand toward him and said, "Come, Holy Spirit, come!" Immediately he began to stagger back, and to the horror of all of us he fell backward on our hard, tile floor with a loud, "Smack!" Everyone who saw this gasped.

In shock, I did not handle this well. I just stood there and blurted out, "Oh no. I look like one of *those*." Everyone knew what I meant. Some chuckled, but I wasn't trying to be funny. In fact, I was embarrassed and not happy about this at all. I had long been critical of television ministers who touched or pointed at people and they fell over. I was very cynical and doubted that what they were doing was really necessary. We were, after all, Church Light. We had no idea what the power of the Holy Spirit was like.

I touched a few more people, and then I noticed that the man who had fallen down was stirring. He got up and began staggering back to his chair. The Holy Spirit said, "I want you to call him back up here and do it right."

I called him by name and asked him to come back to the front. I said that I hadn't handled it well. He looked okay, but as soon as he got close to me he fell over again. Now I was more interested in the process of what was happening. I bent down and asked him, "Are you okay?"

He said, "Yes."

"Has this ever happened to you before?"

He said, "Yes, once before."

"What do you think is happening?" I asked.

"This is the Holy Spirit."

From that point on I lightly touched those who had come forward, saying, "Holy Spirit, bless them." I was hoping nothing else unusual would happen, and it didn't — that night. However, within the next few days the Holy Spirit began really working on me like He had been the last couple of weeks. My hand started shaking when I felt the anointing, and I hid it behind my back so no one could see. Linda didn't even notice it, but I was really uncomfortable.

When I had touched everyone who had come forward, we continued the service as usual. I preached a nice message, and we all went home — many probably wondering for a brief time what had happened. It was such an unusual occurrence that most of us thought it was just a blip on the screen that would never happen again. However, I had made *my third step in my journey toward personal revival. I had invited the Holy Spirit to come into our church services.* I had "gone public."

CHAPTER 4

Rubbing Up Against It

(JOEL)

After the service where I invited the Holy Spirit to come, we went back to business as usual. Privately, however, I continued to experience these unusual times with the Holy Spirit. One evening when Linda and I were visiting one of our home groups, I had a really uncomfortable situation arise at the end. We held hands in a circle to pray, and my hand began to shake again. I quickly took it away and hid it behind my back because I was afraid someone would fall over again. I just did not know what to do with all that was happening to me, and I was pretty frightened about it all. The only thing I could think to do was *the fourth step in my journey toward personal revival. I began to bless the Holy Spirit in anything He wanted to do.* After all, He was God!

I did this knowing that if I went where God wanted me to go in the Spirit, two things would probably occur. First, because of the visions I had had I believed I was going to die to a lot of things and possibly die physically. Second, He was probably going to "blow up" Church Light, and I wasn't sure if that was good or bad. Our reputation as the safe church and my life as I knew it would be obliterated. Therefore, all I could do was to bless Him, trusting that He knew what was best for all of us.

After that unusual Sunday night service, more things happened that I had never experienced before. The Holy Spirit would come on me in my car, and His presence would cause me to weep, cry, or just groan. After a couple of months, I learned to bless this also, which was another big step for me. When I would feel His presence, I would stop what

I was doing and say, "Holy Spirit, I don't know You, and I'm sorry. I just bless You. I just bless what You are doing."

Often when I did this, the Holy Spirit would take me into what I now understand as prophetic intercession. He gave me visions of the lost. I saw the harvest for the first time in my life. I had encounters in the Spirit where I saw people caught in sin, and they didn't know any better. I didn't feel condemnation toward them. I just felt God's heart breaking for them. He would show me homosexuals who were trapped in lies, and He would reveal His heart for them. He would literally take me into weeping. He didn't want to send fire and brimstone to these people. He wanted to save them. He wanted to save drug addicts, gang members, and lost children.

As my heart began to break for the lost and I continued to bless the Holy Spirit for what He was doing, I stumbled into *my fifth step towards personal revival. I actually shared what was happening to me with a friend*. Up until then, I had shared my experiences with no one, not even Linda. I considered all of this stuff private, and I didn't have a language or paradigm for it. I didn't know anyone else who had ever experienced these things, and I didn't know what was happening to me. Because I couldn't explain it to anyone, I just kept it to myself.

One morning I was in my office early and the Holy Spirit came upon me. I stopped what I was doing and said, "Holy Spirit, I just bless what You are doing." The power of God came on me so strongly that I fell to the floor and began to shake in His presence and groan. I took one of the pillows from the sofa in my office and buried my face in it so no one would hear me cry out as I interceded. I thought, *If my secretary hears this she will call 911!*

That went on for about an hour. As the Spirit lifted and I began to come to myself, I began thinking, *Joel, you're losing it. You are just too far out.* Just then the phone rang. I managed to get up and pick up the receiver. My secretary said, "Can you take this call? It's Chris." Chris was a young man from our church who had moved to California to start a Vineyard church there.

Forcing my voice to sound normal, I told her yes. With tears all over my face I said flatly, "Hi Chris."

"Joel, what's happening to you?"

Just then I realized if it was about 8 a.m. our time, then it was about 6 a.m. his time.

I said, "What are you talking about?"

He said, "No, I mean right now, this morning. What is happening to you?"

I thought, *I'm still in the closet. I don't even have a language for this.* And so I lied to him and said, "Nothing."

He said again, "No. No. I mean right now, this morning, for the last hour or two. Something deep is happening to you. The Lord has revealed it to me. Something powerful is happening to you. Joel, what is happening to you? I mean, even just before I called?"

I struggled to keep my composure for a minute and then lied to him again. "Nothing."

He said, "Joel, ever since 4 o'clock this morning when the Lord woke me up, He has been talking to me about what He's doing in your life. Come on, Joel. What's happening to you?"

I started to cry and I said one more time, "Nothing." And then it was almost like I heard a rooster crow and a voice said, "You said, 'Fill me or kill me,' yet you are embarrassed of Me. You are rubbing up against it, but you are being religious."

Chris went on, "Joel, the Lord woke me up this morning and I keep hearing him say, 'Call Joel Budd and tell him, "You're rubbing up against it."' He told me that He wants to sweep across North America and the world in a great outpouring, and you are rubbing up against it. Does this make any sense to you?"

Chris was putting into words what was happening to me in the Spirit, and it was so confirming and liberating to hear him say, "You are rubbing up against it." Totally broken, I wept and said, "I don't want to rub up against it. I want to get in it! I want to get all the way in it! I'm tired of playing safe. I lied to you. I am rubbing up against it!"

Chris said, "Joel, have you heard what is happening in Toronto?"

I said, "No."

"John Wimber called me and said there was something happening at one of the Vineyard churches up in Toronto, near the airport. He asked me and about four other guys if we would go with him and see what's happening up there. We did, and all week it was like I was under an open heaven. It's God! Let me tell you some of the stuff that has happened to me." He told me what had happened to him in Toronto. He described a lot of what had been happening to me and more.

I was out of the closet, and it was time to tell Linda — I wasn't sure what. As soon as I hung up the phone, I left the office and went straight home. I only told Linda that Chris had called, he had told me that something really powerful was happening in the Vineyard church in Toronto, Canada, and John Wimber had said that it was God. Her immediate response was, "Let's go."

We had never gone anywhere like that before. This was the beginning of *my sixth step toward personal revival, pilgrimage.* The next thing I knew, I was in this small church building near the Toronto airport. We got there in the middle of the day, and people were lined up to get in. There were only a few chairs left when we finally entered the building, so we sat in the back. A lot of people were there. The service had not started yet, but already many were crying and groaning and shaking like I had been for the last few months. I was shocked and relieved to see people being touched by the Holy Spirit in the same ways I had been affected in private. I felt a growing sense of relief and excitement. I recognized that whatever the Holy Spirit was doing, I had indeed been "rubbing up against it," and now I was at a fountainhead of the stream I had been drinking from. I began pointing at different people who were obviously being affected by the presence and power of the Holy Spirit, telling Linda, "You see that? I've been touched like that! And see that person over there? That has happened to me!" Linda didn't understand, and I didn't press it.

The next day and night were awesome. There were three speakers, and the last one said, "We can't pray for everyone. There are too many. I want to pray now for people who wrestle with lust."

Linda grabbed my hand and said, "Come on, let's go and get prayed for."

I said, "No, no. That's just for people with lust."

She said, "Oh, *you* lust. Come on!" and she ran off toward the front.

I thought on the way up, *Yeah, I need to be up there.*

Because the speaker had said, "lust," not many came forward and it was easier to get right up in front. But there were still a lot of people in the prayer line. All three speakers came down to pray for the people, and it was like they were in a hurry. The line was long, and if one of them stopped for too long, it would hold up the others coming after them.

The first speaker came by and touched me, prayed a quick prayer, and moved on. The presence and power of God were thick, almost tangible. People were flying all over getting blasted by the Holy Ghost, and Linda fell over next to me, but nothing happened to me. I thought, *Well, maybe the next speaker will do something.* The next guy touched me and prayed a quick prayer and was gone before I knew it, so I began to question myself. *What's the matter with me? Maybe I'm not doing this right. Maybe I do have a lot of lust. Oooooh. Lord, I don't want to lust! I'm sorry! I'm sorry!* I just knew I had to get rid of all this sin before the last speaker came.

The third speaker was going like a freight train down that line. He came up to me, laid his hands on me, and was gone in a flash. Nothing happened, at least not that I could tell. Linda was out of it, so I started back to my seat. As I made my way, stepping over all these people lying on the floor, I noticed that the Prayer Team members were still praying for different ones. They didn't seem to be in a hurry. I knew that was what I needed. I needed someone to take their time with me. Finally a person I will never be able to thank enough came up to me and said, "Could I pray for you?"

I was still a little afraid, but with a new determination I said, "Oh yeah, pray for me." Then I thought, *Okay God, are You going to kill me now?*

As this person prayed for me, I just decided to open up to whatever God wanted to do. It took a little time, but soon I could literally feel the presence of the Holy Spirit. His presence got stronger and stronger until I had to make a decision. I either needed to fight this off or fall down. I couldn't keep standing under the weight of His presence. I decided to surrender and fell back. Then I just laid on the floor, resting in Him. I could hear all the noises and see things if I wanted to open my eyes. I was aware of all that was happening around me. I said, "Holy Spirit, I don't have a clue what You are doing with my life. I don't have a clue what any of this is about. I don't know what's happening around me; I don't know what's happening to me; but I just want You to know that I'm Yours."

Then I heard Him say, "You've never learned to mourn over the lack of intimacy with your earthly father, and I'm going to teach you about a father's love." That was all He said, but that was what He began to do from that day on. Up until that encounter I didn't know I had never experienced the Father's love. He began to teach me about the love that I had never really opened to. He took me through a mourning process and began to heal my wounded, orphaned heart. Although my dad was a great dad, there were six kids in our family, and he was always busy. I only remember being alone with him two times in my whole life, just for a short period of time. We didn't kiss, hold each other, say, "I love you," or express any emotion in my family.

This began a process where the Holy Spirit began to heal me of issues of my past. He took me back through my childhood and teenage years. He showed me that I grew up in a good family, but there was a lack of connectedness and sharing about personal things, including spiritual experiences. We were in church every week, but it was no more important than doing my paper route.

The Holy Spirit also reminded me that there were several occasions when He deeply touched me as a child. I remembered His presence, and how I got saved as a child. Then, when I was a teenager, I became very rebellious and got into sin to the point that my heart was totally hard. I kept my sinful activities hidden from my parents, but my pastor sensed what I was into. At that point in my life my conscience was singed and I didn't have any sense of remorse or conviction — until I met Linda.

Linda was fifteen, had just been saved, and was often asked by the pastor to give her testimony. I was struck by the fact that she really seemed to know and love Jesus, and I was also really attracted to her. In a couple of weeks I asked her out and we began dating. I asked her all kinds of questions about her relationship with Jesus. She hadn't been raised in church and there was no religious phoniness about her relationship with Him. I began to want what she had. It seemed to be real with her.

One night when I was alone, even though I felt absolutely nothing, in faith I told God I was sorry and asked Him to forgive me. But I still felt nothing and heard nothing. About a week later we were in a church service, and at the end, for the first time since childhood, I felt a tremendous drawing from the Lord to go to the front and pray. I went forward, and at the altar He confronted me, "Are you finally going to commit yourself to Me? If I ask you to go to Bible school and become a pastor, will you do it?"

I said, "Yes, Lord."

These were the things that the Holy Spirit reminded me of as He shook my life in Toronto and afterward. It took a while before He dealt with the rape of our daughter, but the time came when He did heal our entire family. All of us experienced a sweet, deeply powerful encounter with our heavenly Father's love, which was the first fruit and most life-changing experience of our encounter with the Holy Spirit. It has become the foundation for everything else. I now realize that I had lived my whole life with an orphan spirit. Now I was experiencing the Spirit of adoption, where we learn to cry, "Abba, Father!"

My pathway of personal revival in the Holy Spirit became my time of getting to know my heavenly Father in an intimate way for the first time in my life. Not only was my heart changing, but my anointing began to skyrocket. Because of my new relationship with my heavenly Father, my life in Jesus Christ went from black and white to Technicolor. Church Light, however, did not like the new colored picture. But before we tell that part of the story, Linda will tell you how the Holy Spirit brought her into the blessing of her Father's love.

CHAPTER 5

"I Can't Stop Shaking"

(LINDA)

I didn't grow up in the church. I grew up in a home that was totally, 100 percent heathen. We never went to church in our lives. My dad was a bitter man, who was emotionally and physically (not sexually) abusive to my mother, my brother, and me. For the things he did to people and to their property, he should have been in prison many times over.

My mother handled all this the way most women of her time did. She just stayed in it. Nobody got divorced. She was a farm wife, had no skills or education to go out and get a job, and relied completely on my dad. She did the best she could and put up with his bad behavior. If she spoke up, many times he would swear at her or hit her, so she didn't speak up very often. All in all, I grew up in a really hard home.

Then my brother got saved. It was the 70s during the Jesus Movement, and lots of teenagers were getting saved. He took me to Joel's church, and I sat there for two months just trying to figure out what they were saying and what was going on. This was so new to me. And I couldn't believe that it was so easy to get to heaven, that all you had to do was believe in Jesus.

Finally, just one month before I turned fifteen, I got saved. I was a shy little girl, but every Sunday the pastor had me give my testimony. While I was giving my testimony, I saw Joel for the first time. He was this rebellious kid with his feet up on the chair in front of him, not caring about anything because he grew up in church and just hated it. But while I was speaking the Lord said to me, "That's the man you're going to marry. You're both going to be pastors, and you're going to have three kids."

I thought, *Well, cool. I'll do that.* You have to understand. That was the first time anyone had cared enough to give me any direction for my life! After that I just knew Joel was going to ask me out, and two weeks later he did. I was the ripe, old age of fifteen, but he kept asking me all these questions about my relationship with Jesus, and I began to see some changes in him. He was getting really serious about the Lord, and then one Sunday night at church he went to the altar and stayed there a really long time. When he came back to his seat he told me that God had called him to go to Bible school. I said, "I know. He already told me."

The change Jesus brought in my life was amazing. Even though I was shy, after I got saved I told everybody in my little farm community about Jesus. They got so they hated to see me coming. The little girl who always hung her head and never said anything was toting a Bible everywhere and hauling to church anyone she could get to go with her. I picked out the worst kids in the school, drove to their farms, and took them to church.

Just as the Lord had told me, Joel and I were married and soon afterward on our way to Bible school. I was eighteen by then. After Joel graduated from Bible school, we began in ministry as associate pastors in a church in Iowa. That was a really good experience for us. The pastors were great people to work for. They loved us and watched over us, and the people of the congregation really loved us also. Joel and I led an evangelism team and got about two hundred people saved, but after seven years God called us to go to Tulsa, Oklahoma, and start Open Bible Fellowship.

We obeyed the Lord, but nobody told me it was going to be so hard. I found Tulsa to be an extremely religious town. There were lots of Bible schools and big churches, but most of the believers were going from church to church instead of door-to-door winning people to Jesus.

I hadn't expected to be a part of a work where nothing really happened, and I became frustrated. I was reading the Word of God. I was having babies. I was at home with my kids and taking care of them because I wanted a happy home. I didn't come from one, and it was really important for me to be at home with my children and raise them right. I would eat beans if that was what I needed to do to stay home with my kids, and that's practically what we did! When you start a church, nobody's helping you and there's very little income.

I wanted to put the Word of God into my kids. I didn't know how to do that, but I figured it out along the way, reading the Bible and teaching them what the Holy Spirit taught me. One day I read Matthew 4:23-24,

> **Jesus went throughout Galilee, teaching in their synagogues, preaching the good**

news of the kingdom, and healing every disease and sickness among the people. News about him spread all over Syria, and people brought to him all who were ill with various diseases, those suffering severe pain, the demon-possessed, those having seizures, and the paralyzed, and he healed them.

That really got my attention. I thought, *Well, if that's what Jesus did, aren't we supposed to do that?*

Then I flipped over and read in chapters 9 and 10,

Jesus went through all the towns and villages, teaching in their synagogues, preaching the good news of the kingdom and healing every disease and sickness. When he saw the crowds, he had compassion on them, because they were harassed and helpless, like sheep without a shepherd. Then he said to his disciples, "The harvest is plentiful but the workers are few. Ask the Lord of the harvest, therefore, to send out workers into his harvest field."

Matthew 9:35-38

He called his twelve disciples to him and
gave them authority to drive out evil spirits
and to heal every disease and sickness.

Matthew 10:1

These twelve Jesus sent out with the
following instructions: "Do not go among
the Gentiles or enter any town of the
Samaritans. Go rather to the lost sheep of
Israel. As you go, preach this message: 'The
kingdom of heaven is near.' Heal the sick,
raise the dead, cleanse those who have
leprosy, drive out demons. Freely you have
received, freely give."

Matthew 10:5-8

After reading Matthew I began reading the
book of Mark, and when I got to the sixteenth
chapter I felt like I couldn't get away from this
stuff. Jesus said,

"And these signs will accompany those
who believe: In my name they will drive out
demons; they will speak in new tongues;

they will pick up snakes with their hands; and when they drink deadly poison, it will not hurt them at all; they will place their hands on sick people, and they will get well." After the Lord Jesus had spoken to them, he was taken up into heaven and he sat at the right hand of God. Then the disciples went out and preached everywhere, and the Lord worked with them and confirmed his word by the signs that accompanied it.

Mark 16:17-20

These verses cut me to the bone, and while I took care of my kids and studied the Word, I was also being the good, little pastor's wife. I prayed for all these people who were needy just like I had read in the Bible, but nothing happened.

Now I'm a real, down-to-earth girl. I see in black and white. And I was getting sick of praying and nothing happening. The church kept growing, but no one was getting saved, and no one was going out to get anyone saved — including me. We didn't even give altar calls at the end of the services! As pastors who reached out to disconnected sheep and sheep that were tired of their present churches, it was easy to forget about those who don't know Jesus. And let's face it, it is uncomfortable to go out in the world and tell the unsaved about Jesus. My excuse was that I was having babies and trying to make a good, godly home for my husband and my kids. But I was still the little girl who told many in high school about Jesus. So I was in conflict over this issue.

Eventually we had all these people coming to our church, but most of them were sick and hurting believers, and everyone wanted counseling. We had become one big, gigantic counseling center. This was not satisfying to me, and I was getting lower and lower when something really horrific happened to our family. We tell about this in another book, but on a family vacation our four-year-old daughter Joelle was raped. It is now a great testimony to God's delivering power, but it was terrible when we went through it. Our elders advised us not to speak of it. Joelle should make that decision as an adult. They meant well, but stuffing all that was terrible for Joel and me.

After this tragedy happened in our family, Joel got desperate for God, and I went from being frustrated to being totally depressed and sad. One day I said, "I've had enough. I feel so low. I've tried to do what the Word says, and it doesn't work. I pray and nothing happens." I was ready to give up ministry and everything to do with God.

I had these thoughts that I just didn't want to be a believer anymore. It was too painful and I felt dead inside. I wasn't afraid of leaving the church and the ministry. I knew that Joel was sharp and could do anything. He could probably make a lot of money and be very happy doing something else. I continued to pray and read my Bible, but my heart wasn't in it anymore.

One day I got a little hope when I read Jeremiah 29:11-13.

> "For I know the plans I have for you," declares the LORD, "plans to prosper you and not to harm you, plans to give you hope and a future. Then you will call upon me and come and pray to me, and I will listen to you. You will seek me and find me when you seek me with all your heart."

I found myself repeating over and over during the day, "You will seek Me and find Me when you seek Me with all your heart."

Then one day Joel came home early from the office and told me about his phone call with Chris. My ears perked up when he said, "Something's happening in Toronto." I didn't understand why something was happening in Toronto that wasn't happening everywhere else because God was every-where, but that was okay. I had been ready to call it quits with God, and this gave me hope. I told Joel I wanted to go and see what it was all about.

Joel told his secretary to call the church in Toronto, and for a month it was crazy. Our secretary told us that every time she got someone on the phone and asked them what was happening up there, they would begin to make noises, laugh, and drop the phone. As a result, we didn't know the address of the church. All we knew from our friend Chris was that it was at the end of the runway at the Toronto airport. We thought, *How hard can that be?* So we got on a plane, flew to Toronto, rented a car, and asked Jesus to show us where to go.

Within twenty minutes we were there, and there was a long line of people. We waited and waited in the line until we finally entered this little, ugly warehouse. Since our building at home was pretty ugly too, I thought, *Evidently God likes ugly places.*

What I saw in that warehouse was nothing like I'd ever seen before in my life. People sat in their chairs and some were crying, making noises, or shaking. Some were lying on the floor crying and making noises. I had no concept of resting in the presence of the Holy Spirit or having the power of God hit me so that I would fall to the floor. Joel had experienced a little of that, but he hadn't talked to me about it yet. The only time I had seen it was on television (which I thought was all fake) and the night Joel asked the Holy Spirit to come and that man fell on our tile floor.

I looked at these people and was in awe. I didn't know what to do. I turned to Joel and said, "Are you supposed to look at them, or do you just look down and pretend like you don't see it?"

He said, "I don't know. Let's just sit down somewhere." As we went to sit down I remembered what I had prayed on the plane, "Okay, God. This is it. If You don't do something for me here, we are done." I knew I was living in a tomb and had to get out.

To this day I couldn't tell you who was preaching or who was leading worship that first service in Toronto. But when I sat down in that place I felt the presence of God for the first time in a long time. I started crying and couldn't stop. I didn't know why I was crying, but it felt good and I didn't care who saw me. I wasn't there for the people; I was there for God.

When the time came for the altar call, we ran up for the prayer line. Nothing happened to us, and I was really sad when we went to bed that night. Even so, the next day we went back and discovered we were at a conference. Since we had never been able to get anyone on the phone who could tell us anything, we didn't know! Evidently we were at a "Catch the Fire" conference. We had made our reservations to stay for a week, and the conference just happened to be the same week.

We also discovered that they were moving to a new building that day because so many people had showed up that they couldn't fit them all in the present building. We helped them move, and they had the next service that night. Again, I can't tell you who was preaching and who was leading worship. All I remember is that when it came time for prayer, there were thousands of people, so I was jumping chairs to get right up there first. Somebody came down the line and touched me, and I went flying. I was literally propelled backwards and fell to the floor.

That had never happened to me before! I thought, *This is really cool!* I was lying on the floor thinking, *I could get up, but other people are just staying down here, so I'm going to stay too.* Then all of a sudden, I began to shake a little bit. I could have stopped it, but I thought, *This feels good, and nobody knows me here, so let's go for it.* Pretty soon my whole body was shaking so much I was coming off the floor. I would have been afraid, but I had been seeking God for so long, and I knew what His Word said about that.

"Which of you fathers, if your son asks
for a fish, will give him a snake instead? Or
if he asks for an egg, will give him a scor-
pion? If you then, though you are evil, know
how to give good gifts to your children, how
much more will your Father in heaven give
the Holy Spirit to those who ask him!"

Luke 11:11-13

I knew God was answering my prayers. The
whole time I shook, I was thinking, *This is really
something.* And then I had a vision, and I had never
had a vision in my life.

CHAPTER 6

Playing with Jesus

You remember that I grew up in a really bad home. I was the only girl and my brother was the only boy. My dad was always telling me I wasn't any good because I wasn't a boy. He needed more help on the farm, and I was just in the way. He would swear at me and tell me I was good for nothing. When I was in the eighth grade he told me I should drop out of school because, "You don't need an education. You're just a stupid girl." This was what I heard constantly, every day.

When I went up for prayer a second time in Toronto, and the Holy Spirit laid me out on the floor, I began to have a vision. I was at a playground, and I was looking at the swings, the merry-go-round, and the teeter-totter. Then all of a sudden Jesus was there, and He said, "Let's play." He led me to the swings and swung me really high, to the point where I thought I was going to fly out of the swing — but I was loving it! He took me on the merry-go-round and spun me so fast. When we were on the teeter-totter He "bumped" me and said, "Isn't this fun?" And during everything He kept looking me in the eye and saying over and over, "I just love you because you're a girl. You are my favorite girl. I made you just the way you are, and you are worth so much to Me."

As Jesus said all these incredible things, it was like a dam broke inside of me. All this emotion began pouring out, emotions I didn't even know were there. When you grow up like I did, you're just tough. You survive. You get over it and get through it or you die.

As I laid there on the floor in Toronto, and Jesus began to heal me of all those years of emotional pain and torment, I realized I had never "gotten over it." I had never gotten over any of it! I had just managed to get through it. Jesus came to me as Father, and Father loved me. He was pouring His love into me. He loved me because I was a girl. He cared about me. He felt bad and cared deeply about Joelle's situation.

I had one vision after another of my past, and Jesus was there making everything right, healing me of all the emotional pain I had stuffed all those years. He reminded me of how He had called me when I was fifteen years old, that He had told me I was going to marry Joel, we would pastor together, and we would have three kids. As He healed me, He refired and reconfirmed my calling at the same time.

All of this started about 9:00 p.m. and by 2:00 a.m. Joel was leaning over me, saying, "Linda, almost everyone is gone, the service is over, and they want to turn out the lights." I tried to get up, but I was shaking so much and was so drunk in the Spirit that I couldn't.

I said, "I'm not leaving. There's no way I'm leaving. I've been looking for this all my life. I didn't know there was anything like this, and you are not getting me out of this now." So he did what any wonderful husband would do. Because I was shaking it was hard to hold onto me, so he grabbed me under my armpits and started dragging me to the door. I protested the whole way, "Just leave me here. I'll stay here in the dark. I don't care."

By this time I was afraid that if I left the church Jesus and the presence of the Holy Spirit would go away. This was the most awesome thing that had ever happened to me next to getting saved, getting married, and having my kids. I felt Jesus touching me, kissing me, loving me just the way I was. He was telling me that I was good, that I was special to Him. And I was like a drug addict getting high for the first time. I was totally addicted to Jesus — and frightened of losing this depth of experience with Him if I left the building.

I told Joel again that he had to leave me there, that I couldn't get up and walk anyway, but somehow he managed to get me out of the building. He set me on the sidewalk and went to get the car. I saw him pull up, get out, and he sort of threw me into the car. He buckled me into my seat belt and went around to get into the driver's seat. We drove to the hotel, and he pulled up to the front door like a gentleman and said, "Okay, get out and I'll go park the car." Of course, I couldn't even unbuckle my seat belt, so he pulled around to the parking garage, parked the car, pulled me out of the car, and began to drag me into the hotel.

He really began to see how funny this was as he dragged me through the hotel lobby toward the elevator. There were lots of people even though it was the middle of the night, and when we got into the elevator he just laid me on the floor, shaking. Other people in the elevator were staring, and in concerned voices they said something to him. Unfortunately, they were speaking French, and we couldn't understand them. I got tickled at this and started laughing. Joel didn't know what to do, so finally he just threw up his hands and said, "I can't take her anywhere!" Then he started laughing too.

When we got to our floor, the elevator doors opened and he dragged me to our room, propped me beside the door, and said, still laughing, "See you later!" He put the key in the door and said, "I've got to go to the bathroom. Stay here." Like I could go anywhere! There I was in the hallway, by myself, shaking and not caring at all. Soon he was back, laughing and thinking he was so funny. He dragged me into the room and threw me on the bed. The bed was vibrating so much from my shaking that he said, "You are not sleeping in the bed," and he put me in a chair near it. Then he surrounded me with pillows, thinking that if I shook so much that I fell out of the chair, I would fall on something soft.

I was enjoying what God was doing in me, but the shaking was still a shock. Remember, all I had known was Church Light. Joel must have been concerned about me, because he sat on the bed and began to tell me for the first time everything that had been happening to him. I looked at him amazed as he told me about the visions of the train and the plane and the lost, the groaning, the shaking, falling on the floor, and crying out for the lost. He told me the whole story about the phone call with Chris and said, "We are rubbing up against something that God wants to do in our generation and all over the world."

I said, "Whoa! Well, all I know is Jesus is real to me for the first time since I got saved. I don't care if I'm shaking. I'm going to die like this because I never want this to go away. This is so real. I didn't know there was anything like this. Jesus is touching me. He's telling me He likes me. I can't get enough of Him. And something's changing inside me. Bad stuff is coming out of me and good stuff is going into me. So don't worry about me. You just go to sleep."

Joel laid down and pulled the covers over himself. It wasn't long before I slid out of the chair and onto the floor. I laid there all night. I can tell you the time the sun came up in the sky. In the morning I reached up and pulled on the covers, saying, "Wake up, Joel. It's time to go back to the church." I got him out of bed and said, "Help me get in the shower so we can go back," and we were back at the church at nine o'clock that morning. That is what we did every day of the conference.

Amazing things happened during those days of romping around the spirit realm with Jesus. At one point I got up and started running in place for two hours. I like to run, but this was different. Jesus said to me, "I'm putting something in you that you can run the race for the long haul."

I just went with it.

When it was time to go home, of course, I didn't want to go. By this time I was absolutely drunk in the Spirit most of the time, and I knew Jesus was doing something wonderful in my life. I missed my kids, but that was the only reason I wanted to go home. When we got on the plane, I really needed the seat belt because I was still shaking. The airline attendant wanted to know if I was okay. I said, "I've never been better!" I began to notice that I was somewhat of a spectacle, but I didn't care. God was touching me.

As the plane began to take off Joel held my hand and looked at me very seriously. Finally he said, "Linda, I've been through some church splits in my life. I've grown up in the church, and churches split over lesser things than the way you look right now. If this continues, people at the church may not understand it. They might not like it."

At that point I didn't understand what he was saying. I didn't grow up in church. I had no real concept of religion or legalism or traditions of men.

I said, "Why wouldn't they like this? This is Jesus. This is the best thing that ever happened to me next to getting saved. I mean, I was ready to tell the Lord good-bye, and look what He's done! Why wouldn't they like this?"

He squeezed my hand and said, "Let's take a vow that we won't back away from this no matter the cost. If we have to start over in our home again with a few people, we will."

My eyes opened wide and I began to get it. I was thinking, *Oh man, I don't want to do all that again!* But we squeezed each other's hands and said we would do that if that's what it took to keep this incredible new intimacy with God in our lives. We had had a taste of the love of the Father and the joy of knowing Jesus as our best friend, healer, and deliverer. There was no way we were going to give that up — no matter what it cost us.

Little did we know that *we were going to walk through fire because we were carrying the fire.*

CHAPTER 7

Willingly Paying the Price

(LINDA)

By the time we landed in Tulsa I was still shaking, and I didn't fully understand that Jesus was shaking all the pain, shame, guilt, depression, and discouragement right out of me. All I knew was that I was feeling a whole lot better. Unfortunately, because we didn't fully understand what the shaking was about, we couldn't explain it to anyone else.

At that time our girls were fifteen, twelve, and six years old. When we got home and they saw us — especially me, shaking — at first they were curious.

I said, "I met God!" and Joel put them at ease by explaining that Jesus was touching me. Then he made it fun for them. He said, "Hey kids, just go up to Mom and say, 'Holy Spirit. More, Lord, more.'"

They said, "Okay," went up to me, touched me, and they had just said, "Holy Spirit," when He came on me so strongly that I fell under the power and shook more. After that they relaxed and just thought it was funny. Now I was a big rag doll they could play with and drag all over the house! They were old enough to understand that God was doing something good to their mom — and to fix their breakfast if I was shaking too much to do it!

We had returned on Sunday, and the next day we went to the church to meet with our staff. They were anxious to hear what had happened to us because they knew that we had gone to receive something from God. I continued to shake as we told them our story, and the Holy Spirit began to move on them as they sat in their chairs. Some began to cry. Others began to shake a little. When it came time to break for lunch, we said, "We want to pray for you, but we don't want to pressure you. So go to lunch, and if you want us to pray for you after lunch, just come back to this room and we will."

They all came back and asked us to pray for them. To our amazement, the Holy Spirit began to move on them just like He had moved on us! In Toronto Pastor John Arnott had told us that we were going back carrying something for our people, but when he had said that, we just pictured Church Light and thought, *No way! They will never get this.* But now his words were proving to be true. After praying for the staff and seeing what God did, we began to understand that we *were* carrying something powerful.

We began to wonder what would happen when we went to church on Sunday. We decided to tell our story, and that would be the sermon. At eight o'clock Sunday morning Joel opened the door of the church for me. The shaking had worn off a little bit, but the minute I heard the praise and worship team rehearsing I fell in the Lord's presence and began to shake again. Joel dragged me from the doorway into the church, and the worship team cried, "What's wrong with her? What happened?" He just told them I was fine and that they should keep practicing. Then he put me on the chairs in the front row.

In the past I had been very shy and afraid of being in the pulpit. The most I had done was give a few announcements. But that day I said to Joel, "I want to help you today. I want to tell people what has happened to me." When the time came, Joel helped me as we climbed the stairs of the platform together.

Our church at that time was filled with highly educated people. Oral Roberts University's medical school was still there, and we had about eighty medical students in our church as well as many professors and students. We said we were a charismatic church, but there wasn't anything charismatic going on. We were just a bunch of Christians getting together to sing some nice songs and hear a nice message. We helped a lot of people with their dysfunctional relationships in counseling and taught biblical principles to help them be successful, but our services didn't allow the Holy Spirit to move at all.

When we got back from Toronto, all that changed. There we were on Thanksgiving Sunday 1994, standing on the platform. I was shaking, and for the first time I was telling our congregation more than just a couple of announcements. "We've been pastoring you now for eleven years, and you didn't know this, but we were really weary and tired because nothing ever happens here. Nobody ever gets saved. You all came from other churches because you got tired of those churches. Pretty soon you're going to be tired of us and go someplace else. Nobody gets healed. We don't even talk about it. Nobody ever gets delivered of demons because we all believe that there aren't any in America.

"We were so tired of nothing happening, and then we heard there was an outpouring of the Holy

Spirit in Toronto, Canada. When we got there, we found people shaking under the power of God, just like I am now. And we'd never seen it before, but we knew that it was God, that it was real, and we had to have Him. We needed for Him to turn our lives around and cause us to feel like we were in touch with Him."

After I said that, we asked the Holy Spirit to come. Our congregation, who never said anything but just sat quietly and took notes, began to stand, cry out, and fall out of their chairs. It began on one side of the church and moved all the way to the other side. Then something really wild happened. There was a group that always came to church together and they had a leader. This man didn't like what was going on and got up to leave, so everyone in his group got up to leave too. As they moved toward the doors, the Holy Spirit fell on them, and they went down. The leader, who was rather heavy, fell to the floor, and as he did his pants came down a little. He continued to crawl toward the door, and the more he crawled the more his pants slid down his backside!

We didn't know about prayer cloths, and no one knew what to do. He began sobbing, did an about face, and started crawling up the aisle toward the front, dragging his pants. When he was almost to the front of the church, he motioned with his hand that he wanted the microphone. Someone gave him a microphone, and he said, "I know this is God, but I hate this! I was trying to get out of here. I know this is God in this place, but I don't want anything to do with it. And because of that, God pulled my pants down. He's just...taking all...the pride... out...of...me." His friends didn't come to the front, but they didn't leave either.

Joel and I were just holding on to each other, trying to keep standing, and watching this happen. We looked at each other in complete shock and didn't know what to do. Then we remembered how John Arnott had just kept saying, "More, Lord. More." So that's what we said, and then we were falling over and people were running to the front crying, "Help me, Jesus! Forgive me! I'm sorry, Jesus!"

We always had two services on Sunday mornings, and we had to make sure the first service ended in time to clear the parking lot for the second service. The first service was the deader of the two, so that was never a problem — until the Sunday after we returned from Toronto. It looked like a war had happened in our building. Bodies were all over the floor, people were groaning and crying out to God. We told them they had to leave to make room for the second service, but a lot of them couldn't move.

When the people came for the second service, they walked in the doors and said, "Whoa!"

We told them, "It's okay. Just come in, step over people, and we'll explain what's happening." Then we kept on asking God to give us more.

Our worship team went through their songs like they always did, and I was on the floor again. When they finished Joel and I made it up the stairs to the platform to tell the second service what we had told the first service. God is so funny! He did the same thing in the second service that He did in the first service. From one side of the church to the other people began crying out, falling down, and then either running to the front or running for the door. Wherever they went, we knew the Holy Spirit was touching them.

This kept going on until the afternoon, when we finally said, "Why don't you go home? Come back for the evening service, and we'll start again." Everyone who wanted more came back at six o'clock, and the service lasted until one o'clock in the morning. It was incredible! That's what we thought, anyway.

The next morning one of our elders called and said, "Linda, you are an embarrassment to us. We can't bring visitors here anymore. You need to stop this."

I said, "You know what? I'm sure I am, and I'm really, really sorry. But I can't stop shaking, and even if I could stop it I wouldn't because I've gotten hold of Jesus. He's real and I'm not letting go of Him."

From that time on, every week our church of one thousand began dwindling down. By December all of our elders had quit. In two months we were at six hundred members. Many were leaving and saying mean things to us, but I continued to be camped out on the floor with Jesus. I began to realize that the Holy Spirit was not a "gentleman" in the way we had always been taught. He could touch you as deeply as He wanted without your permission. He could move on you and cause you to be fully overcome by Him whether people approved or not.

I began to really live all the scriptures like Romans 8:17, which says, "Now if we are children, then we are heirs — heirs of God and co-heirs with

Christ, if indeed we share in his sufferings in order that we may also share in his glory." That's what I had always wanted, to share in His glory! It was okay if I went through suffering because I knew His resurrection power and glory were going to be the result of it.

We had now pastored a total of eighteen years, seven in Iowa and eleven in Tulsa, and everything we believed about having church had been turned upside down by the Holy Spirit. But from the time of the conference in Toronto, every day I felt better and better. The shaking continued nonstop for nearly two years, and Joel had to sleep on the couch for awhile, but years of pain in my childhood and the agony of what we had gone through with our Joelle began to flow out of me and go away forever. Jesus was more real than ever. Depression slipped away in defeat. Life looked good again, and our future had a hope despite the consequences of all of this. God was everything to us now.

CHAPTER 8

The Fire of My Father's Affection

(JOEL)

Many of those we considered our good friends in the church left without saying a word. A few others did tell us they were leaving. Interestingly, the number one comment we heard was, "I know this is the Holy Spirit hitting our church, but I don't like it." Our great reputation in the community was now not so great. A famous minister across town preached against what was happening in our church during his radio program, giving false or exaggerated reports, and we became famous in a "different" way.

We began to see that before we went to Toronto we had been so conservative, so afraid of stepping out in the Spirit, and we had surrounded ourselves with people like ourselves. Our members were conservative, and they liked the fact that we were so conservative. Some of them eventually had become very frustrated and bored like we had, but others liked Church Light and were really upset when it was destroyed by the Holy Spirit.

We didn't understand why the Holy Spirit came to our church like a freight train and a fighter plane, so we clung to the scriptures that said that He would teach us and comfort us. And He did. One of the first things He showed us was that when you are led by the Holy Spirit, He will take care of you. We didn't have to start over with twenty people in our home. The more people left, the more our finances increased.

He also began to give us comfort about this mass exodus of people. He showed us that believers were at different places in Him, and we have no right to judge that. If they leave our church, then that is between them and Him. We are simply to do what He has called us to do and bless them as they go.

He led us to start a monthly Friday night renewal service, and new people started coming to check out what was happening. We weren't sure where this was heading, but we knew He was taking care of us. After experiencing the anointed, intimate worship in Toronto, we were frustrated with our shallow worship services; so it was during one of these Friday night services that He dealt with our worship leader. She had been wonderful for Church Light, and we really loved her, but she made it clear that she hated what was going on now. Again and again we talked her out of quitting.

At the very beginning of the renewal service one evening, she got up to lead worship, and it is important that you know she had a microphone with a cord. As she began to sing the power of God hit her. She began twirling and twirling from one side of the platform to the other. We were thinking,

She's going to fall off! She kept screaming, "Help me! Help me!" But God just kept twirling her until finally she fell down with the cord wrapped around her like a mummy!

Both of us were afraid to go up on the platform. This was a manifestation of God's power. It was a sign and a wonder. We were thinking, *God has wrapped her up in it!* I finally got up to try to lead worship while others carefully unwrapped her. We were singing an upbeat praise song and people were still arriving when a little boy about two years old came walking up the middle aisle to the front. When he was just about to the stairs of the platform, he looked back at his mom, who was coming for him. She was concerned that he was going to be a distraction.

The little boy saw his mom, smiled, and began to bounce up and down to the music. When he did that, we all broke loose and began to dance. We thought, *"This is cool. A little child shall lead them!"* (Isaiah 11:6). That was the day that Open Bible

Fellowship of Tulsa began to dance with Jesus. It was a small beginning, but eventually it became a common experience.

As soon as our worship leader was free of the cord, she got up and then fell over under the power of God again. Eventually, she got up, but she was unable and unwilling to lead worship again. The next morning she quit. Before she left, however, she said, "There's a guy in the congregation who's been coming here for a couple of years. He does the kind of music you guys like, the kind of music they do at the Vineyard churches. His name is Darrell Evans."

The next day Linda was out running and the Lord spoke to her, "I want you to hire Darrell Evans. I want you to give him a chance."

That same morning while I was exercising, Darrell's face flashed in front of me. It surprised me. I had a sense of God's peace and felt we were to hire him, even though we had never heard of him or seen him lead worship. This was different for us!

When Linda came home, I said, "I've got to tell you something. The Lord just told me we're supposed to hire Darrell Evans."

We met with Darrell right away. He told us the things that had happened in his life, and where he was spiritually. We said, "Well, do you feel like you're supposed to do this?"

He said, "Yeah. I feel like I'm supposed to do it."

We said, "Okay, we'll give you a chance."

The next Sunday he was on the platform and he led in a totally different style. He was a hang-loose, go-with-the-flow type of guy. The band he inherited, however, had charts and a song order. "Flowing in the Spirit" musically or any kind of spontaneous worship drove them crazy. They all left, but we encouraged Darrell that his music was really anointed. "Just keep getting plastered in the Father's love with us, and if He gives you new songs, just sing them." Encouraged by our faith in him, he went out and brought in other musicians and singers who could flow with him and the Holy Spirit.

Things were changing. From that time on we would preach what the Holy Spirit was teaching us and then ask for the presence of God to come. People would get powerfully touched and would soak in His presence while ministry took place. Darrell would sit and play during the entire service. As the Holy Spirit came in power, he began writing songs. During one service he said, "Hey, folks. I'm getting something from the Lord." He strummed his guitar and turned to the band to say, "Stay with me, guys."

At this point our congregation was not yet freely dancing. Therefore, I was a closet dancer. I would dance at home, while I was mowing the lawn with my headset on, and in my prayer time. The Lord was really setting me free, and I was having a great time even though I didn't know how to dance. My idea of dancing was mostly just bouncing up and down like a bunny.

When Darrell began strumming and told us the Lord was giving him something, the Holy Spirit said to me, "Dance for Me." I struggled for a moment because I had never gone public in dancing before the Lord. Then I decided to go for it. As I began to step out I heard, "You'll lose five more families if you do this." The place was packed out and I had always had a battle with the fear of man. On top of that, I had bone spurs in both feet, and they were really bad. I had been to several doctors, and it had gotten so painful that I could hardly walk.

I said, "Lord, You know about the bone spurs and You know I can hardly walk, let alone dance. All I will do is bounce like a bunny and look really stupid — and was that You who said I would lose five more families?" All the while Darrell is strumming and waiting on the Lord for the song.

Then I heard it again, "Dance for Me."

I wrestled and wrestled inside until finally I told Linda.

She said, "Go for it!"

I yelled, "Yes, Lord! Yes, Lord!" and began bouncing all over the place.

Darrell immediately yelled, "That's it!" and started singing, "Yes, Lord! Yes, Lord! Yes, yes, Lord!" That song came out in a prophetic, spontaneous rush and became known as, "Trading My Sorrows." And the next morning when I got out of bed, I discovered that God had healed my feet!

What we began to understand was that when the Holy Spirit moves and we move with Him, all kinds of amazing things happen. People get healed inside and out. They begin to feel the love of God their Father, they get to know Jesus as their very best friend, and they begin to fully trust the Holy Spirit to lead them in every area of their lives. Then there is this burst of creativity that comes directly out of the Father's love. New songs. New ideas. New desire to reach the lost and help the poor.

Our church began to grow again, and we settled into a continual longing for more of Jesus. Those who were hungry and thirsty like we were joined us. When we heard that other ministries and churches were experiencing what we were experiencing in the Spirit, we visited them. Some were in the city of Tulsa, some were in other states, and some were in other countries.

Richard Roberts had Rodney Howard-Browne as a speaker at Oral Roberts University. We went, and Rodney Howard-Browne prayed for us seven times that day. We were completely drunk in the Spirit, as were many of the people and students. A couple of weeks after that Benny Hinn came to town to have a big crusade. We sat in the middle but at the end of our row. All of a sudden during praise and worship Benny Hinn walked down from the platform, down the aisle, looked at us, and said, "Fresh!" And we got totally refreshed again!

Every place we went, the Holy Spirit seemed to zero in on our hunger. He touched us and healed us and destroyed us all at once. Then we heard what was happening in Brownsville, so we took a pilgrimage there. We heard about the Argentina revival from Cindy Jacobs, who invited us to go with her, so we went down to Argentina. Randy Clark invited us to go with him to Mozambique, Africa, to minister to their leaders with Roland and Heidi Baker. Once again we received an impartation by the revival anointing these leaders carried. We just kept experiencing more and more of the Father's love and power. It was in these places of revival that the leaders also imparted to us a passion to reach the lost out of the overflow of the Father's love.

CHAPTER 9

Community Transformation

About three years after we went to Toronto, I was in intercession at a Monday evening prayer meeting, I found myself on the floor with my arms crossed. I began to cry because of how far we had come as a church. Then I had a vision that I was a mummy in a tomb. I was all wrapped up in the grave cloths, and I was trying to get out. I was scared and crying, and the Lord said, "There are people that are still coming into this place who are wrapped up like mummies. They're dead inside like you were, and they want to break out. I'm sending them to Open Bible Fellowship because there is an anointing here for that. When you lay hands on them, they're going to break out of their mummy clothes."

I spent some time in intercession, knowing that people were getting free as I prayed. Then one of our pastors took the microphone and said, "Isn't this wonderful tonight? I believe that we've really broken through to a new level of freedom tonight. And I believe that a lot of us have been praying for those who are struggling to get free. There are some people that the enemy would like to take out of the church because they're just to the point of getting free. We need to *fight* for them tonight." She said exactly what I had been hearing from the Lord and praying!

Then the Lord spoke to me and said, "Share this message so that those who aren't sure will keep coming back to be touched, and those who have been touched will keep coming back for more. There is so much more! Share this message so that all of you can be on the same page. In these three years I have brought to you a people who are your people now, and I'm going to raise up leaders because I have a great work for you to do. I'm drawing the people together as a body instead of just a bunch of strangers."

At this point we had come together as a congregation. We were being refreshed by Father's love. We were falling down, repenting, shaking, and getting whole in Him — but we were not moving.

The next Sunday I shared all this with the entire congregation and told them it was time to get moving. All this freedom and power we were experiencing was not just to make us feel good. We were getting healed, delivered, and set free to get other people saved and healed and delivered and set free. Once we get free, we can turn our attention to other people and what they need from the Lord. And when we move forward and help others, we need to stay filled with the Holy Spirit. We need to keep coming back for more and more of Him because the more of Him we have, the more of Him we can give.

A few years before I had had this revelation, just after we had been to Brownsville, I had come home and set up a stage in a nearby low-income apartment complex. I had the worship team sing and play, and then I preached the gospel. People started getting saved, strange people began coming to our church, and the members of Church Light who were still with us as well as some new people didn't like it. They criticized me and I stopped. Then a while later we went to Argentina and experienced the great revival that was going on there. Thousands were being saved, and we both got fired up to get out there and do the works of Jesus.

What I had read about years ago in Matthew and Mark — what I had longed to do and had previously been unable to do — we were now determined to do. Now being filled with the Father's love, I was no longer afraid of what people would think about me. He had yanked all that fear out of me. We knew this was what God had called us to do, and that it was a direct outgrowth of knowing the Father's love. When you know the Father's love, and you flow in the Father's love, the most natural thing is to give it away to others, especially to lost and hurting people. That is the Father's heart: to make you whole and then to use you to help others become whole.

We started reaching out for the first time to the struggling neighborhoods around our church. Instead of longing to move into a more wealthy, prestigious neighborhood as we had during Church Light, we now had a love for people from all walks of life around us. About that time a Wal-Mart closed in our area, a place with a lot of space, and God led us to buy it. We started an additional ministry called Harvest House, which is a place where people can come for food and clothing, bus tokens, and other things. So we needed a large place for that outreach.

We went to a public elementary school in the middle of our poor neighborhood, and invited them to what we called the "Christmas Connection." We asked the school to make a list of all the kids who probably wouldn't get any presents and find out what they wanted and needed. Then we had a big Christmas party at the church, passed out their gifts, played real Christmas music, and preached the gospel. Many were saved, their lives changed for the better, and the kids do much better in school.

The authorities of the school were so blessed by what we did, and they were so impressed by the difference in the children's lives, that they have allowed us to come in every year to invite the children to our church for the annual Christmas Connection. They see us as a neighborhood philanthropic organization, and our relationship with them has expanded.

We offer more help to the kids who need it. We give them free eye exams and eyeglasses, dental exams, doctor visits, haircuts, tutoring — anything they need. Now the school lets us come over and have movie nights and do all kinds of things to bring Jesus to their kids. Every year on Halloween we throw a big party at our church, inviting all their kids to come. The teachers tell their students, "Don't go trick-or-treating in the neighborhood. It's too dangerous. Go to Open Bible Fellowship because you'll be safe, you'll have a lot more fun, and you'll get a lot more candy." Our church's neighbor kids come flooding in because it is a safe and fun place to be.

We established the Firestorm School of Ministry, which teaches believers to do everything that Jesus did while He was on earth. They learn to share the gospel of the kingdom, heal the sick, cast out demons, move in the gifts of the Spirit, and even interpret people's dreams. Then we send them out in outreach teams to practice what they have learned. We have booths at fairs where people can come for physical healing, a word from the Lord, or the interpretation of their dreams. We are out there taking all the psychics' business away from them! The people not only get answers to their problems, but they encounter the Father who loves them and the Savior who died for them. We are also teaching all this to our teenagers and our children. Even our Sunday school kids know how to heal the sick and cast out a demon!

During our Church Light years, if we had met the woman at the well, we would have never talked to her. Caught in all her sin and poverty, she would have intimidated us or disgusted us. Back then, we just wanted acceptance by wealthy, successful people. We didn't care about the lost, the hurting, or the needy. Today, we are sons and daughters of our Father and are acting more like it. When we meet the woman at the well, we have a word of knowledge from the Spirit to open her heart, we have the love of the Father to capture her heart, and we have the authority of Jesus, the Living Truth, to set her free.

We tremble in fear when we think what we would have missed if we had resisted God's drawing and never said, "Come, Holy Spirit, please come!"

CHAPTER 10

There's Always More!

(JOEL AND LINDA)

It has been twelve years since our first trip to Toronto, and today we are even more passionate about receiving more and more from the Lord. We are always excited to see believers excited about knowing Him and serving Him. But we also have to fight the disappointment when we see so many get heavy, religious, and stuck in a rut. They can hang around revival but never get in it. We've seen it over and over in our church. There are all kinds of people who like to just "rub up against it." They like to watch it and hang out on the corners of it. They like to laugh and say, "Oh, that's great! Isn't that wonderful? Somebody got saved. Somebody got healed. Somebody got touched." But they never jump in the water themselves.

The bigger danger we have seen is that after awhile they get bored with it because they aren't being refreshed and refired themselves. Then they stand on the sidelines looking for things they can criticize instead of looking for the good that God is doing. They get religious and critical and don't realize that they are refusing what the Holy Spirit is offering them. They are literally refusing freedom, joy, intimacy, and a new passion for the things of God — unknowingly going back under the influence of a religious spirit.

Many also don't realize that God is not only shaking us — He is shaking the world. Earthquakes, hurricanes, tsunamis, wars and rumors of war are happening all over the earth. That's not an accident! We are living in a time when the church must be full of fresh fire, God's power, His Word, and His love. It is not the time to stop asking for more. We have a world to reach!

One day we were getting ready to go out of town to minister when something that had never happened in our house suddenly occurred. Now, when something unusual happens these days, we just automatically think prophetically, *What is God saying in this?* To us, being prophetic includes always having eyes to see and ears to hear what God is saying about our lives and then saying it and doing it.

We live in a large house because our children, who are all grown, still live with us. Therefore, in this large house we have an amazing alarm system that includes state-of-the-art smoke detectors. That day, as we were throwing our stuff in our suitcases and getting ready for our trip, all the different smoke alarms and heat detectors throughout the house went off. Now the manual that we have for this alarm system says that this is not possible, but nevertheless it was happening.

The sound was so deafening that the dogs and cat were running for cover, and Linda ran out of the house to try to get away from it. Her first thought was, "God, what does this mean?"

She heard the Holy Spirit say, "You are going to start more fires. Are you ready for more?" She knew that we were going to see the fire of God come even more than ever before in our lives and through our ministry.

Those who know us may have looked at us and said, "More? Haven't you had enough already?"

So many believers, even in our own church, believe that you get touched by the Holy Spirit now and then — whenever He feels like it — and that's it. They come to our church, experience the power and presence of the Holy Spirit, get touched, and then leave. They never come into the understanding that there is always more!

God can't take us from faith to faith and glory to glory if we believe He just touches us every once in a while. We must stay in that place of expecting and receiving from Him all the time. He is always "downloading" love, revelation, or prophetic instruction. The Holy Spirit is a Teacher, and teachers love to teach! He is always wanting to tell us what we need to know about our Father, our Lord and Savior and King and Priest, Jesus, and how He wants to work in us and through us.

Just like we love to hang out with our kids, the Holy Spirit likes to hang out with us. There are times when He just wants to soak us in His love, fill us with His peace, and invade every cell of our being to heal us and transform us. We love all these experiences with Him. We love it when He teaches us. We love it when He heals us. We love it when He tells us what's ahead of us. And we love it when He expands the capacity of our hearts to give and receive more of our Father's love. We love what King David said, "You have anointed me with fresh oil and given me the strength of a wild ox" (Psalm 92:10, my paraphrase). We need that strength and freshness!

There is no end to the new stuff you can receive from God. There is always more! We know we will never get it all in this life, and it will probably take eternity for us to take in everything God is and has for us. That's why we get somewhat frustrated with believers who get a touch from God and think that's all there is. There is so much more!

Ask, Seek, Knock

If there is one thing we know for certain, it is that nothing much is going to happen to you spiritually if you don't hunger for more of God. That's why we have written our story, to provoke you to new levels of hunger and longing to know your Father more and more intimately — and never stop getting to know Him.

Jesus talked about this at length, and Luke records what He said.

> Then he said to them, "Suppose one of you has a friend, and he goes to him at

midnight and says, 'Friend, lend me three loaves of bread, because a friend of mine on a journey has come to me, and I have nothing to set before him.'

"Then the one inside answers, 'Don't bother me. The door is already locked, and my children are with me in bed. I can't get up and give you anything.' I tell you, though he will not get up and give him the bread because he is his friend, yet because of the man's boldness he will get up and give him as much as he needs.

"So I say to you: Ask and it will be given to you; seek and you will find; knock and the door will be opened to you. For everyone who asks receives; he who seeks finds; and to him who knocks, the door will be opened.

Luke 11:5-10

Jesus said, "Suppose *you* have a friend." Who is Jesus talking to? He's talking to *you*. This is about *you*. If you put yourself in this story as Jesus wants you to, that means at midnight a friend from out of town stops by to spend the night. He is hungry and you have nothing in the house to feed him. You are powerless to help him, so in desperation you go to another friend for help. But this other friend does not want to be bothered and tells you to go away. He's too tired. It's too late. After all, everyone in the world is in bed asleep!

We are here to tell you that the church is waking up because God is shaking us. He is opening our eyes to see that the world is getting bolder and bolder about asking, seeking, and knocking! The people with the needs are going to keep coming to our doors. They are going to be hungry and thirsty and naked and sick and poverty-stricken. They will persist and continue beating upon our doors until their boldness wakes us up to meet their needs through the awesome, loving power of Jesus Christ.

Believers who are already answering this call are saying, "Lord, I don't know if I can do this anymore. I'm tired, it's midnight, and I want to rest in my bed and spend time with my family." But as the end of the age approaches, the hunger for Jesus is only going to increase, in the world and in the church. And the truth is, the hunger for the Lord should be greater in the church, among us who already know Him and have tasted and seen that He is good.

In these last days a wave of hunger for God is going to hit the earth, and we need to be even hungrier so that we will have an abundance of the Bread of Life to give to those who are asking, seeking, and knocking. They will come to us at midnight and at noonday and at every hour, and we must be ready for them.

Remember, Jesus is talking to *you!* That means *you* must be asking, seeking, and knocking boldly to receive everything He wants to give *you*. You can be bold because He has already told you that everyone who asks gets what they ask for, everyone who seeks finds what they are looking for, and everyone who knocks has doors opened to them that are far beyond their wildest dreams. So what are you waiting for! Start asking, seeking, and knocking!

Proverbs 1:32 says, "The complacency of fools will destroy them." Renounce complacency and begin to ask afresh, to seek afresh, and to knock afresh. The lost and those hungry for more of God are going to come, and if you don't have that refreshing for yourself from the Lord, they will wear you out like so many babies in your bed!

The Father Wants You to Have It

Jesus goes on to say,

> "Which of you fathers, if your son asks for a fish, will give him a snake instead? Or if he asks for an egg, will give him a scorpion? If you then, though you are evil, know how to give good gifts to your children, how much more will your Father in heaven give the Holy Spirit to those who ask him!"
>
> Luke 11:11-13

We have seen some of the most self-centered people on earth become parents and, although they stay self-centered, when their kids nag them for something they give it to them. This is a picture of the most dysfunctional family and yet even selfish parents still give stuff to their bratty children. Jesus is saying, "If evil parents give to their rebellious children, how much more will your loving heavenly Father give to you, His child, made righteous and holy by the blood of His Son?"

There is always more of Him to know, and we can never get to the end of God's love, truth, and power. It is time for believers to ask, seek, and knock like crazy to be filled and filled and filled again with the Holy Spirit and the revelation of God's heart for us. This is something the Father wants to do! He wants to give the Holy Spirit to those who ask Him. He wants us to be so tanked up on Holy Ghost love and power that when we encounter the lost we will be fully prepared and even ecstatic to give them everything they need from Him.

If you are not hungry, if you do not feel thirsty, it is time to ask the Holy Spirit for help. Get in a church where the presence of the Holy Spirit is manifesting in authentic and tangible ways and the fresh revelation of God's Word goes forth in love. You can never get enough of God's Word, yet it is not how much of the Word you know that will satisfy you or make you a lover of God or people. Ask the Holy Spirit to help you experience the Father's affection for you and remain hungry for what He longs to feed you from His Word.

Buy a new praise and worship recording and relight the fires of worship in your heart. Get in a Bible study where you can get your mind transformed with God's Word. Hunger begets more hunger, so hang around other believers who are hungry and thirsty for God.

Recognize and repent of the dry, lifeless places in your spiritual life. Ask the Holy Spirit to come and reveal the spirit of adoption, the Father's affection for you. Ask Him to touch you deeply, give you new vision, and impart a fresh anointing. We can tell you from years of experience that since we have jumped into and determined to stay in the river of God — the flow and power of the Father's love — our lives and our ministry have been transformed. We are more productive, more creative, more refreshed, more joyful, and more effective. And the best part is that we know our Father's love and have our Father's heart.

We realize now that all the gold, silver, and precious stones God was talking about in His Word begin and end with His love. When we have His love and operate in His love, we act like Him. Jesus said that He came to show us the Father. He said, "Anyone who has seen me has seen the Father. How can you say, 'Show us the Father'?" (John 14:9). He went on to say in verse 10 that everything He did was from the Father. When we walk with the Father and experience His love for us, we just naturally become more like a son or daughter, like Jesus, and do the same things Jesus did.

Experiencing the Father's love and giving it away is the difference between a dry, dead, religious life of service and the abundant life of peace, joy, wisdom, and miracle-working power Jesus died to give you. If you long to know the Father's love, desire to do the works of Jesus, and want to be fully empowered by the Holy Spirit, pray this prayer with us now:

"Holy Spirit, I want to experience the love of my Abba, Father. In Jesus' name I renounce an orphan spirit and an orphan heart. I invite the Spirit of adoption to manifest in my heart, mind, and emotions starting right now.

"Father, I now believe with my whole heart that You chose me and adopted me in Your heart. I now come into agreement with the Spirit of adoption and ask You to kiss my heart awake to Your wonderful affection for me. I receive Your love, in faith, as You promised. I welcome and receive Your kisses of love on my heart! Kiss me again and again until my heart burns with Your sweet affection for me, for my brothers and sisters, and for all those who don't know You. In Jesus' name I pray, amen."

About the Authors

Joel and Linda Budd have been the senior pastors of Open Bible Fellowship in Tulsa, Oklahoma, for the past twenty-three years. The Budds have pastored for a total of thirty years and have a rich experience in the things of the Spirit. They teach that believers owe the world an encounter with God, and a gospel without power and love is not the gospel that Jesus preached.

The Budds founded and oversee the Firestorm School of Ministry, where believers learn to break off strongholds that hold back confidence, freedom, and anointing. Students learn to discern spirits, lead people in deliverance, heal the sick, and prophesy in the marketplace, at the workplace, and in the local church.

Whether the Budds minister individually or together, the hallmark of their ministry includes physical and emotional healing and deep encounters with the Father's love and power. They partner with and minister in many other churches that are also seeking authentic revival. This relationship network crosses denominational lines, helping emerging leaders walk together in purity of heart and the Father's love and power.

Pastors Joel and Linda live in Tulsa, Oklahoma, with an assortment of pets and two of their three daughters, Cristin and Haley. Their daughter Joelle and husband David Burris live in Tulsa as well.

To contact Pastors Joel and Linda

you may write:

Pastors Joel and Linda Budd

Open Bible Fellowship

1439 East 71st Street

Tulsa, OK 74136

or call:

918-492-5511   *Ext 39*

or e-mail:

lindab@obftulsa.org

Weekly sermons and teaching

by Pastors Joel and Linda

are available on the church website:

www.obftulsa.org

Other Materials From Pastors Joel and Linda Budd

Soon to be released . . .

No Longer Bound

In this book Pastors Joel and Linda tell what they learned about spiritually guarding their children from the attacks of the enemy. They give the heart-wrenching account of the rape of their four-year-old daughter Joelle, the agony and hardship they endured, and the gracious goodness of the Lord to heal them as a family. This book is a must for every Christian parent because we all have a divine destiny to fulfill, and the devil will try to bind your family in some way to keep you from being happy and successful.

So You Want to Date My Daughter?!

With three grown daughters, Pastor Joel Budd gives other parents the benefit of his wisdom and experience in dealing with the issues of dating. This book is the outline he and his wife Linda used for their daughters and those who dated them. If you are wondering how to joyfully and successfully navigate the dating years, this resource is a must. Tested over the years by other grateful dads and moms — and young people — it has gotten rave reviews from parents and kids alike. See for yourself how fun, clear, and clean the dating years can be.